BOXER
FUN IS OUR BUSINESS

www.booksbyboxer.com

Bee Three Books

Bee Three Publishing is an imprint of Books By Boxer
Published by
Books By Boxer, Leeds, LS13 4BS, UK
Books by Boxer (EU), Dublin, D02 P593, IRELAND
Boxer Gifts LLC, 955 Sawtooth Oak Cir, VA 22802, USA

cs@boxer.gifts

MADE IN CHINA
ISBN: 9781915410627

FSC MIX Paper FSC™ C007683

This book is produced from responsibly sourced paper to ensure forest management

YOUR BROTHER WANTS TO LEAVE THE BAND?

LIAM'S ADVICE:

SMASH HIS GUITAR.

THAT'LL MAKE HIM STAY. (IT DIDN'T)

WHAT WOULD YOU DO IF YOU MET AN ALIEN?

LIAM WOULD

"TELL IT TO F*CK RIGHT OFF BECAUSE WHATEVER PLANET HE CAME FROM, THEY WOULDN'T HAVE THE BEATLES"

-2017

SEEN A GAGGLE OF GEESE?

LIAM'S ADVICE:

SAY,

"ALRIGHT, GEEZERS?"

- 2017

FEELING HUNGRY?

WHATEVER YOU DO, DON'T COOK.

LIAM HATES COOKING, AND

"COOKING CAN F*CK RIGHT OFF."

FEELING DOWN?

LIAM'S ADVICE:

"JUST LOOK IN THE MIRROR AND GO:

'WHAT A F*CKING GOOD-LOOKING F*CK YOU ARE.'

AND THEN I BRIGHTEN UP."

HOW DID LIAM SPEND HIS CHILDHOOD?

"JUST PLAYED FOOTBALL AND COME IN LATE FOR ME TEA AND KNOCKED ON PEOPLE'S DOORS AND RUN OFF.

RUN THROUGH PEOPLE'S BACK GARDENS AND PINCH THINGS."

WANT TO GO TO GLASTONBURY?

LIAM ONLY GOES

"FOR THE MONEY"

BECAUSE HE

"F*CKING HATE[S] GLASTONBURY."

- 2004

WHAT SHOULD YOU DO AFTER AN AWARDS CEREMONY?

LIAM'S ADVICE:

GO TO OXFORD STREET AT 3 AM AND GET

ARRESTED.

LOOKING FORWARD TO THE BANK HOLIDAY?

HOW SWEET.

FOR LIAM,

"IT'S ALL ONE BIG BANK HOLIDAY, ONE BIG F*CKING DAY OFF."

DO YOU HAVE A FAVORITE CEREAL?

LIAM'S ADVICE:

EAT IT SO MUCH THAT IT BECOMES YOUR NICKNAME.

HIS WAS

'WEETABIX'.

HEAVEN OR HELL?

WELL IF THE DEVIL HAS

"GOOD GEAR"

AND GOD HAS

"THE INSPIRAL CARPETS AND NUNS",

FOR LIAM, THE CHOICE IS CLEAR!

LIAM'S ADVICE TO A$AP ROCKY:

HE SHOULD CHANGE HIS NAME TO

'WHATSAPP RICKY',

BECAUSE

"THAT'S A BETTER F*CKING NAME ANYWAY."

- 2017

YOU'RE ON HOLIDAY, WILL YOU GO FOR A SWIM IN THE SEA?

LIAM'S ADVICE:

DON'T DO IT, THE SEA ISN'T MEANT FOR HUMANS, JUST

"SHARKS, AND THE JELLYFISH, TADPOLES AND STUFF."

GOING BALD?

LIAM WOULD NEVER BE SEEN ON STAGE AGAIN, AS "THERE'S NO PLACE FOR BALDNESS IN ROCK AND ROLL." HE'D INSTEAD "CHOP ME HEAD OFF."

WHAT DOES LIAM THINK PEOPLE THINK OF HIM?

"THEY THINK I'M A BIG-MOUTHED C*NT FROM MANCHESTER, AND THEY'D BE CORRECT."

IS SOMEONE THROWING SOMETHING ON STAGE?

LIAM WOULD TELL THEM

"IF YOU DON'T LIKE THE MUSIC,

F*CK OFF!"

LOOKING TO CHANGE CAREER?

LIAM'S ADVICE:

"BE GOD, MAYBE? THAT WOULD BE A GOOD JOB."

- 2005

DOES LIAM MIND PEOPLE LOOKING IN HIS BINS?

HE THINKS IT'S A GOOD THING BECAUSE IT GIVES HIM A

"KICK UP THE ARSE. OTHERWISE [HE'D] JUST BE SAT AROUND GETTING FAT."

- 1997

WHAT SHOULD YOU DO ON CHRISTMAS?

LIAM'S ADVICE: JUST SIT THERE ALL DAY

"GETTING WANKERED... EATING LOADS OF F*CKING FOOD AN' ALL."

HOW SHOULD YOU DO YOUR GARDEN?

LIAM'S ADVICE:

HE MUCH PREFERS IT TO BE

"F*CKING PAVED."

PLAYING A BIG CONCERT AT A FAMOUS VENUE IN L.A?

LIAM'S ADVICE:

ACCIDENTALLY DO CRYSTAL METH INSTEAD OF COCAINE, PLAY AN AWFUL SET, THROW A TAMBOURINE AT YOUR BROTHER, AND AFTERWARDS RUN OFF INTO THE NIGHT.

IS LIAM DOWN WITH HIS FEMININE SIDE?

"WITHOUT A F*CKING DOUBT."

DOES LIAM DANCE?

NO.

HE **REFUSES** TO DANCE. HE "CAN'T DANCE ANYWAY AND [HE'S] NOT IN A BAND FOR THAT."

ARE YOU FEELING COLD?

LIAM'S ADVICE:

DON'T WEAR A CARDIGAN.

HE HAS A "BIT OF AN ISSUE WITH CARDIGANS. THEY'RE SH*T, AREN'T THEY?"

SHOULD YOU GO TO A GIG TONIGHT?

LIAM'S ADVICE:

"F*CK THAT.

WHAT'S THE POINT?

THE BANDS ARE ALL SH*T, AREN'T THEY?

GO OUT TO SOCIALIZE AND HAVE SOME STUDENT STAND ON YOUR

F*CKING SHOES?"

ARE YOU MELLOWING WITH AGE?

SO IS LIAM.

"BUT NOT IN THE SENSE OF LIKING RADIOHEAD OR COLDPLAY."

- 2008

WOULD LIAM SELL HIS WEDDING PHOTOS TO A MAGAZINE?

HE'D HAVE TO BE

"WELL AND TRULY F*CKING DESPERATE."

LIAM'S ON STAGE PLAYING TO THOUSANDS OF PEOPLE. WHERE DOES HIS MIND GO?

"THE PRICE OF BEANS IN YUGOSLAVIA."

WOULD LIAM MOVE TO IRELAND TO AVOID TAX?

"THAT'S FOR GREEDY C*NTS. I LIKE THE TAXMAN. THE TAXMAN'S GOOD."

SETTING AN ALARM?

LIAM'S ADVICE:

MAKE SURE YOU WAKE UP A MINUTE BEFORE YOUR ALARM CLOCK GOES OFF,

"JUST TO DO ITS HEAD IN."

HEADING TO PLAY YOUR FIRST OVERSEAS GIG?

DON'T DO WHAT LIAM DID:

HE GOT IN A BRAWL ON THE FERRY, GOT ARRESTED, AND THEN DEPORTED BEFORE EVER MAKING IT TO EUROPEAN SOIL.

AT LEAST IT WAS

"PUNK ROCK, MAN."

ARE YOU GETTING ENOUGH SLEEP?

IF YOU ARE, THAT'S FAR TOO MUCH. LIAM SAYS HE "F*CKING HATE[S] SLEEPING" AND WISHES HE DIDN'T HAVE TO BECAUSE HE'D "RATHER BE UP, LIVING."

DO YOU WANT KIDS?

LIAM'S ADVICE:

HAVE

"20! SELL 16 AND KEEP FOUR!

TAKE THE EYEBROWS OFF, THOUGH, THEY DON'T COME WITH EYEBROWS!"

PLAYING TWO HISTORIC CONCERTS AT KNEBWORTH?

LIAM'S ADVICE:

FORGET THAT YOU'RE DOING TWO NIGHTS AND GET BLACKOUT DRUNK AFTER THE FIRST. SO MUCH SO, YOU NOW CAN'T REMEMBER ANYTHING.

DOES ANYTHING SCARE YOU?

LIAM IS SCARED OF

"MICE."

FROM 73 QUESTIONS WITH VOGUE, 2020

THINKING ABOUT LEARNING TO PLAY THE SAXOPHONE?

THINK AGAIN.

"THEY'RE A BIT CREEPY AREN'T THEY...

I DON'T LIKE THEM AND THEY'RE A BIT PERVY I THINK.

SOMEONE GETS A SAX OUT AND YOU KNOW THERE'S SOMETHING GOING DOWN."

- 2017

WANT THE ICONIC LIAM WALK?

IF YOU'RE NOT FROM MANCHESTER, YOU'RE OUT OF LUCK. ACCORDING TO LIAM, THE WALK COMES FROM MANCUNIANS HAVING

"LONGER ARMS THAN ANYONE ELSE. AND WE WEAR BIG COATS, AND IT JUST DRAGS OUR ARMS DOWN A BIT."

- 2003

PLAYING AT ABBEY ROAD, THE HOME OF YOUR HEROES, THE BEATLES?

DON'T DO WHAT LIAM DID:

HE AND OASIS GOT BANNED FROM THE STUDIO AFTER BLASTING OUT THE BEATLES AT

FOUR IN THE MORNING.

WHAT WOULD LIAM DO IF HE SAW A POLITICIAN TAKING DRUGS?

"I'D GIVE THEM A CRACK ROUND THE HEAD...

'WHAT ARE YOU DOING,

YOU DONUT'"

- 2020

IS YOUR BROTHER AT THE STUDIO, RECORDING?

LIAM'S ADVICE:

BRING A GROUP OF STRANGERS YOU JUST MET AT THE PUB TO WATCH YOUR BROTHER, AND GET IN AN ARGUMENT WITH HIM TO THE POINT HE SMASHES YOU OVER THE HEAD WITH A

CRICKET BAT.

LATER, SELL THE BAT AT AUCTION.

WOULD OASIS HAVE BEEN A SUCCESS WITHOUT NOEL?

LIAM POSES THE MORE IMPORTANT QUESTION,

"WOULD JESUS CHRIST HAVE BEEN A

F*CKING PERVERT

WITH A CRISP PACKET ON HIS HEAD? NO ONE KNOWS."

- 1997

TIME FOR BED, WHAT SHOULD YOU WEAR?

LIAM'S ADVICE: WEAR YOUR "SUPERMAN OUTFIT".

- 2022

WHO WAS ONE OF LIAM'S HEROES GROWING UP?

THE INCREDIBLE HULK, BECAUSE HE "LIKED HIS GREENNESS."

WHAT'S YOUR GUILTY PLEASURE?

LIAM'S IS

BLUR.

FROM 73 QUESTIONS WITH VOGUE, 2020

WHAT IS GOING TO HAPPEN TO YOUR BODY WHEN YOU DIE?

LIAM'S

"GOING TO BE

MUMMIFIED

AND PUT ON DISPLAY IN A MUSEUM."

WHAT IS LIAM LOOKING FORWARD TO ABOUT PLAYING WITH HIS BROTHER AGAIN?

"BLOWING HIM

KISSES

IN BETWEEN EACH SONG."

EVER WONDERED WHO THE

PATRON SAINTS OF MANCHESTER

ARE?

ACCORDING TO LIAM, THEY'RE

"SHAGGY AND SCOOBY DOO."

- 2003

WHAT WOULD LIAM DO IF HE MET GEORGE HARRISON?

HE'D

"STAND ON HIS HEAD AND PLAY GOLF."

- 1998

WHY DOES LIAM USE TWITTER?

BECAUSE HE

Liam Gallagher

@liamgallagher

"LIKE[S] WINDING PEOPLE UP...

WITHOUT A DOUBT, THAT'S WHAT IT'S ALL ABOUT, YOU KNOW WHAT I MEAN?"

- 2017

VISITING NEW YORK?

LIAM'S ADVICE:

DON'T SPEND MUCH TIME DOWNTOWN, BUT SPEND A LOT OF TIME IN

CENTRAL PARK.

"I'VE GOT TO BE BY TREES, OTHERWISE I GET CLAUSTROPHOBIC."

SEEN

LIAM GALLAGHER?

LIAM'S ADVICE:

DO:

ASK,

"ARE YOU THE ONE AND ONLY LIAM GALLAGHER"

AND APPROACH HIM BOWING.

SEEN

LIAM GALLAGHER?

LIAM'S ADVICE:

DON'T:

SAY,

"HELLO, NOEL."

WHAT IS LIAM'S LIFE MOTTO?

"LIVE IN THE NOW."

WHAT WOULD YOU DO IF YOU MET GOD?

LIAM'S ADVICE:

"I'D GIVE HIM A KICK IN THE BOLLOCKS AND SAY: 'WHAT THE FUCK ARE YOU DOING, LETTING ALL THESE YOUNG KIDS GET KILLED IN ALL THESE WARS AND STUFF?' "

WANT TO START APPRECIATING MUSIC MORE?

DON'T DO WHAT LIAM DID:

HE ONLY LIKED MUSIC AFTER HE GOT HIT IN THE HEAD BY A HAMMER WHEN HE WAS ABOUT 15/16.

BEFORE THAT, HE ONLY CARED ABOUT FOOTBALL, BUT

"A COUPLE OF WEEKS LATER, MUSIC STARTED CREEPING IN."

WHY WOULD IT BE A BAD IDEA FOR LIAM TO ASK JOHN LENNON QUESTIONS?

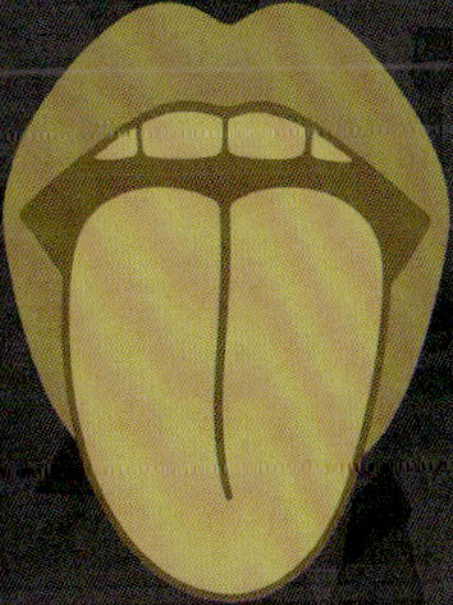

"BEFORE YOU KNOW IT, I'D END UP LICKING HIS FACE."

- 2003

GETTING A DIVORCE?

LIAM'S ADVICE: COVER UP THE TATTOO OF YOUR EX WIFE'S NAME WITH AN ELVIS TATTOO,

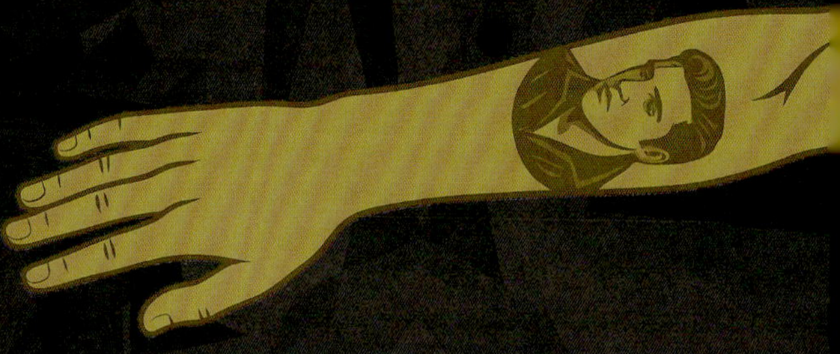

"BECAUSE HE'S COOL."

IS YOUR BROTHER GETTING WOUND UP IN AN INTERVIEW (THE AUDIO OF WHICH WOULD REACH

52 IN THE CHARTS)?

LIAM'S ADVICE: TELL HIM TO

"SIT THE FUCK DOWN,

YOU'RE GETTING INTO A STATE, YOU'VE HAD TOO MANY

G&TS."

WHAT DOES LIAM THINK OF HIS LOOKS?

"I'M A PRETTY BOY, YEAH.

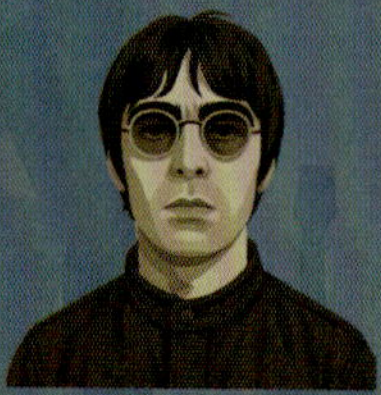

YEAH, I'M PRETTY GOOD-LOOKING.

I TAKE CARE OF ME HAIR.

BIT **OBSESSED** WITH ME HAIR.

YOU GOTTA HAVE A DECENT HAIRCUT IF YOU'RE A FRONTMAN."

AT A HOTEL BAR IN MUNICH?

DON'T DO WHAT LIAM DID:

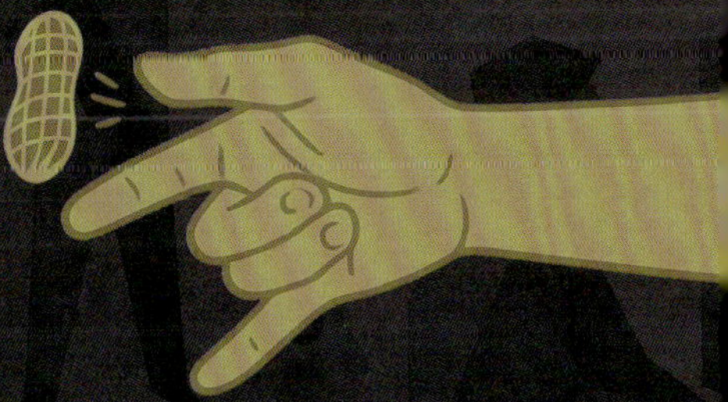

HE SUPPOSEDLY FLICKED PEANUTS AT A RANDOM GROUP OF MEN UNTIL THEY BEAT UP HIS SECURITY AND HIM, KNOCKING OUT TWO OF HIS FRONT TEETH.

WHO WERE YOU IN A PREVIOUS LIFE?

DESPITE HIM DYING WHEN LIAM WAS 8,

"JOHN LENNON."

- 2003

ARE YOU A BIT BIG HEADED?

IT'S FINE - LIAM HAS ALWAYS HAD A

BIG HEAD.

HE'S

"A BIG-HEADED ARROGANT BASTARD."

BUT HE NOW HAS

"A RIGHT."

DO YOU?

THINKING ABOUT GETTING A PET?

LIAM'S ADVICE:

GET AN ALSATIAN AND CALL HIM HENDRIX.

SO YOU CAN

"HOLD HIS HEAD AND STARE INTO HIS EYES, SEE WHAT HE'S THINKING."

- 1998

GETTING A NEW HAIRCUT?

LIAM'S ADVICE: GET A

"TERRYBARRYGARRY PERM. ALRIGHT?"

- 2000

FEELING HUNGOVER?

LIAM'S ADVICE: GO

"STRAIGHT BACK TO THE PUB, NO MESSING ABOUT...

DON'T SIT AND DWELL ABOUT IT, HANGOVERS, JUST GO STRAIGHT BACK AGAIN AND IT'LL JUST WORK ITSELF OUT."

- 2020

WOULD LIAM DO A SWIMSUIT SHOT?

"YEAH! SPEEDO. LUNCH BOX HANGING OUT, DUNCAN GOODHEW CAP ON. TOTALLY, MAN."

CAN'T FIND THE LIGHTSWITCH WHEN YOU'RE DRUNK AND NEED A PISS AFTER YOUR

FIRST NIGHT OUT?

LIAM'S ADVICE:

JUST PISS ON YOUR OLDER BROTHER'S NEW STEREO, BECAUSE

"WHEN YOU GOTTA GO, YOU GOTTA GO, YOU KNOW WHAT I MEAN?"

SOMEONE SHINING A LAZER PEN AT YOU DURING YOUR SHOW?

LIAM'S ADVICE:

CALL HIM A "F*CKING COCKNEY DARTH VADER"

AND TELL HIM IF HE DOES IT AGAIN YOU'LL

"COME DOWN THERE AND STAB [HIM] IN THE THROAT WITH ME CREDIT CARD."

ARE YOU SCARED OF DYING?

LIAM'S NOT.

"IF I DIED IN 0.2 SECONDS I WOULDN'T GIVE A F*CK BECAUSE I'VE HAD IT - I'VE HAD A GREAT F*CKING TIME."

- 2016

DON'T HAVE ENOUGH ENERGY?

YOU SHOULD HAVE DONE WHAT LIAM DID AS A CHILD AND

"ATE TOO MUCH WEETABIX. SIX EVERY MORNING. WITH ALL THE SUGAR ON TOP."

YOUR BROTHER MENTIONED YOUR £1000 FINE FOR FIGHTING ON A FERRY?

LIAM'S ADVICE:

TELL HIM,

"YOU CAN STICK YOUR THOUSAND POUNDS RIGHT UP YOUR F*CKIN' ARSE 'TILL IT COMES OUT OF YOUR F*CKIN' BIG TOE."

WATCHING THE MUPPETS?

LIAM'S FAVORITE IS

"KERMIT THE FROG, INNIT."

WHAT'S YOUR SPIRIT ANIMAL?

LIAM'S IS DOLPHINS.

FROM 73 QUESTIONS WITH VOGUE - 2020

SHOULD YOU GO FOR A NIGHT OUT?

LIAM'S ADVICE: NO, GOING OUT IS BORING AND HAS BECOME SH*T. HE'D

"RATHER STAY AT HOME WITH THE CURTAINS CLOSED, PUT THE CANDLES ON."

- 1998

THINKING OF MOVING ABROAD?

MAYBE FOLLOW IN LIAM'S FOOTSTEPS?

"I'M GOING TO MEXICO TO MAKE HATS."

- 2000

NERVOUS TO PERFORM?

LIAM'S ADVICE: NO YOU'RE NOT.

YOU'VE NEVER BEEN NERVOUS ABOUT A CROWD, JUST BELIEVE:

"IF I DON'T DO IT, NO ONE ELSE WILL."

WHAT SHOULD YOU HAVE FOR BREAKFAST?

LIAM'S ADVICE:

NOT TOAST.

HE DOESN'T

"EVEN MAKE TOAST ANYMORE."

HE

"BANNED IT."

- 2020

HOW DOES LIAM FEEL ABOUT GETTING A ROCK'N'ROLL REPUTATION?

HE'S INTO IT... BUT AT THE END OF THE DAY, HE GOES

"HOME AND GET[S] A CLIP OFF ME MAM."

WHAT KEEPS LIAM DOWN-TO-EARTH?

"BEING ME.

BEING LIAM GALLAGHER KEEPS ME

DOWN-TO-EARTH."

(YOU MIGHT HAVE TO TRY SOMETHING ELSE!)

SOMEBODY THREW A FISH ON STAGE?

LIAM'S ADVICE: ASK

"WHICH D*CKHEAD THREW THE FISH HERE, THEN?

STINKY, SMELLY FISH MAN.

LISTEN MAN, I AIN'T THAT F*CKING BAD, DON'T BE THROWING FISH...

I CAN'T BE SINGING WHILE THERE'S A FISH THERE."

TOURING OR NOT TOURING?

BACK IN 1995, LIAM

"HAD A MONTH OFF IN JANUARY, AND IT DONE ME HEAD IN."

DOES LIAM UNDERSTAND WHY HIS BROTHER DOESN'T WANT TO GET THE BAND BACK TOGETHER?

NO.

"HE'S ACTING LIKE I STABBED ONE OF HIS CATS, OR I SLAPPED ONE OF HIS KIDS, OR, DARE I SAY IT, TRIED IT ON WITH HIS MISSUS."

- 2020

HAS PAUL MCCARTNEY OFFERED YOU A MARGARITA?

LIAM'S ADVICE:

ASSUME HE'S TALKING ABOUT MARGHERITA PIZZA AND TELL HIM YOU'RE NOT HUNGRY BECAUSE YOU'VE ALREADY EATEN.

BAR ABOUT TO CLOSE?

LIAM'S ADVICE: TIME TO ORDER

"THREE DOUBLE JACK DANIELS AND COKES, AND THREE BEERS, MATE."

- 1995

SOMEONE UPSET YOU SLAGGED OFF THEIR BAND?

LIAM'S ADVICE: TELL THEM TO

"F*CKING GO BACK TO ART COLLEGE, YOU LITTLE WUSSIES."

- 2006

MET IDRIS ELBA?

LIAM'S ADVICE:

THROW HIS HAT ACROSS THE BAR BECAUSE HE MESSED UP YOUR HAIR WHEN HE HUGGED YOU.

WOULD LIAM ARGUE WITH HIS BROTHER IF THEY WEREN'T IN A BAND?

OF COURSE HE WOULD.

"IF WE HAD A GREENGROCER'S, GALLAGHER'S GREENGROCER'S, WE'D ARGUE OVER WHICH WAY WE SET OUT THE APPLES OR THE F*CKIN' PEARS."

- 1995

GOT BANNED FROM AN AIRLINE AFTER YOUR BEHAVIOR ON A FLIGHT TO AUSTRALIA?

LIAM'S ADVICE: DOESN'T MATTER.

"I'LL TELL YOU KIDS... I'D RATHER WALK."

FEELING LONELY?

LIAM'S ADVICE: THERE'S NO POINT.

HE

"CAN'T BE ARSED WITH ALL THIS HAVING LOADS OF PEOPLE TO PLEASE"

AND

"YOU DON'T NEED MATES WHEN YOU HAVE KID."

SHOULD YOU DO YOGA?

LIAM'S ADVICE:

"LAYING ON YOUR BACK AND ALL THAT, GETTING INTO BENDY AWKWARD POSITIONS?

NO, I DON'T THINK SO...

NO, NO YOGA FOR ME."

- 2006

WHAT DOES LIAM FIND TO BE THE HARDEST PART OF THE ROCK N' ROLL LIFESTYLE?

"STAYING TRUE TO YOURSELF AND KEEPIN' IT REAL."

- 2020

YOUR BROTHER JOKED THAT HE OWNS YOU?

LIAM'S ADVICE:

GRAB A CHAIR AND LOB IT AT HIM.

WHAT IS LEFT FOR LIAM TO CONQUER?

"IT'S NOT A QUESTION OF CONQUERING, NOT AT ALL. WE'RE JUST GOING TO KEEP MAKING MUSIC

'TIL WE DIE.

AND IF WE CONQUER ANYWHERE... CONQUER?!

F*CKING STUPID. WILLIAM THE F*CKING CONQUEROR?

'OFF WE GO, DON'T FORGET THE BEANS!' "

- 2000

ARE YOU WORRIED ABOUT DEATH?

LIAM'S ADVICE: YOU SHOULDN'T BE.

"I'VE ALREADY DONE IT BEFORE. DONE IT A COUPLE OF TIMES AND IT'S A

PIECE OF PISS.

THERE IS NOTHING TO IT, YOU JUST SIT THERE AND WAIT FOR IT TO HAPPEN. BIG DEAL."

WHO IS HE?

"I'M **LIAM GALLAGHER**

AND I'M IN

OASIS.

THE WHOLE WORLD IS JEALOUS OF ME.

IT SHOULD BE."